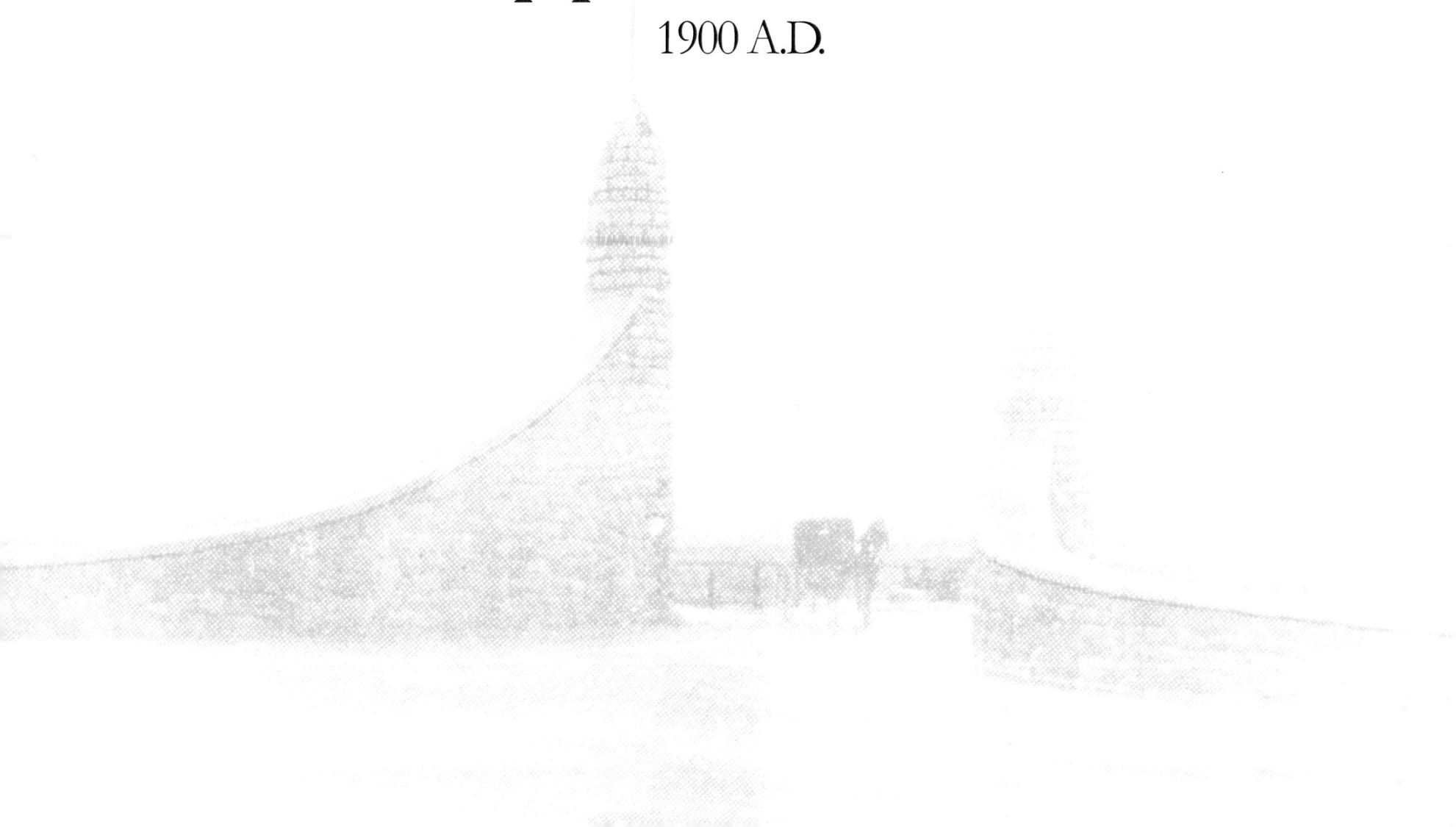

HOWARD!

1900 A.D.

Original texts by Henry A. Jones, M.D., from "The Dark Days of Social Welfare at the State Institutions at Howard, Rhode Island," published in 1943 by the Department of Social Welfare.

This attribution serves to duly recognize the original author and source. The purpose of this book is to pay homage to the profound insights and scholarship of Dr. Jones, and to ensure their continued dissemination and appreciation.

www.theladdschool.com

HOWARD!

1900 A.D.

Foreword: An Invocation

Just over six miles from the heart of Rhode Island's capital, near a now vanished stretch of the abandoned Pawtuxet Valley Railroad line, a place called Howard resides stoically on the fringes of the city. Once a quiet farming hamlet with a simple rural charm, it was perched at the southern slope of Sockanosset Hill, overlooking the woodlands and farmlands of early Cranston. Here, the William Howard farm, around which the eponymous village grew, embodied all the quaintness of a pastoral existence; a stark contrast to the burgeoning needs of a state grappling with the daunting challenges of poverty, crime, and mental illness.

In the mid-19th century, this contrast would set the stage for an extraordinary transformation. With the purchase of the adjoining Stukely Westcott and Howard farms for the establishment of a House of Correction and Asylum for the Insane Poor, the State Institutions at Howard began to take shape. Marking the first foray into a statewide, publicly administered approach to social welfare, this State Farm would become the cornerstone for Rhode Island's efforts to centralize the care and custody of the insane, indigent, criminally convicted, and feeble-minded.

But the developing situation at Howard in the decades that followed marked a dramatic departure from its founding ideals. As one century gave way to the next, the grim realities of chronic overcrowding and unsanitary conditions overshadowed the initial promises of reform. Diseases, like the outbreak of tuberculosis which first ravaged its population in 1887, brought not only suffering but also numerous deaths, epitomizing the dire struggle against the harsh conditions within these institutions. The once-aspired sanctuaries, conceived to rehabilitate, increasingly descended into turmoil, overwhelmed by the afflictions they were meant to alleviate.

Today, Howard stands as a vastly different landscape. Absorbed into the urban sprawl and overshadowed by modern infrastructure, its historical significance is a whisper among the clamor of progress. Where once stood reformatories, now lie modern structures and bustling highways. Government offices and commercial centers occupy the grounds where asylums and prisons once provided refuge and rehabilitation. The former State Infirmary, with its granite towers, now serves new purposes in a changed world. Yet, in these spaces, the presence of Howard's past still lingers; a shadow cast by an era long ago.

The photographs in the pages that follow open a window to this past, revealing scenes of a history lost. Sourced from a diversity of archival materials, hand-colored, and digitally restored, each image is imprinted with the distinct character of its age and origin, and indelibly marked by the tangible signs of time's passage. Presented alongside them are the words of Dr. Henry Aaron Jones, the State Infirmary's first medical superintendent, whose insights likewise illuminate the darkest corners of these institutions; the Asylum for the Insane, the Sockanosset School for Boys, the Oaklawn School for Girls, the State Prison, and State Almshouse.

Together these pages conjure a vision of light and shadow made whole, vividly realized and fully manifested by the invocation of 'Howard!' shouted from the early morning train.

Reception Hall

"Howard! Howard!" — What memories the name awakens. Memories of the ball and chain, the sullen prisoners with closely cropped heads, in dirty gray uniforms; the locked step, the downcast eye that showed, by its baleful and furtive glance, the seething mental condition of the mind that had not found itself and was tortured by the expressions, "Justice", which was, to the wretched prisoners, a mockery, and its very sound an echo to them of "Man's inhumanity to man."

It was a chilly, April seventh morning that I first saw Howard. There had been a light fall of snow, through which the emerald green of a patch of winter rye on the prison farm, near the depot, sent up its green lance blades toward the clouded sky. The snow was damp and stuck to one's feet and very soon penetrated the rubberless shoes of the gang of prisoners, slopping along in the field near the railroad. The morning train from Providence on the Pawtuxet Valley branch of the New York, New Haven and Hartford Railroad, held a peculiar looking, motley crowd of people. Many of them, to my immature knowledge, were not very joyous in appearance, and when the conductor, standing in the doorway, shouted out, "Howard — Howard," I found the reason.

Many of them had looked with despairing eye through the car windows to what to me appeared to be a stately castle of gray stone, oval-windowed, massive and turreted, and architecturally attractive; but to these in this car, it was the grim castle of despair, the place of sorrow, of resignation, and of death!

I was startled to see the train disgorge itself. Out upon the wet snowy platform, a handcuffed group were hustled, slipping and clanking down the slippery steps of the car. Calls and shouts from sheriffs in blue uniforms straightened up this motley crowd into a semblance of order, save one poor female, who, clanking her shackled wrist as one would a bracelet, screamed out some unintelligible language which showed she was insane.

Upon getting out on the platform before the prisoners came out, I was pleased with the toy depot and its bustling depot master. Growing alongside of the depot towered a beautiful white birch tree, where from the very topmost bending limb was a bright splash of red, the early robin, from whose throat poured out in thrilling notes its clear melodious tones of hope and gladness, the first sweet harbinger of spring. The noise and conflict of the human throng, however, frightened it away. The song of hope and gladness died as it had died in the minds of some of those prisoners, nearly, then, out of my range of vision.

No flag was flying, emblazoned with the legend, "Hope." This, to them, was a thing of the past, for they had reached what appeared to them their last depot and final destination.

"It was Howard."

Congregate Dining Hall

Waiting Room

Reception Hospital Hallway

Man Sitting

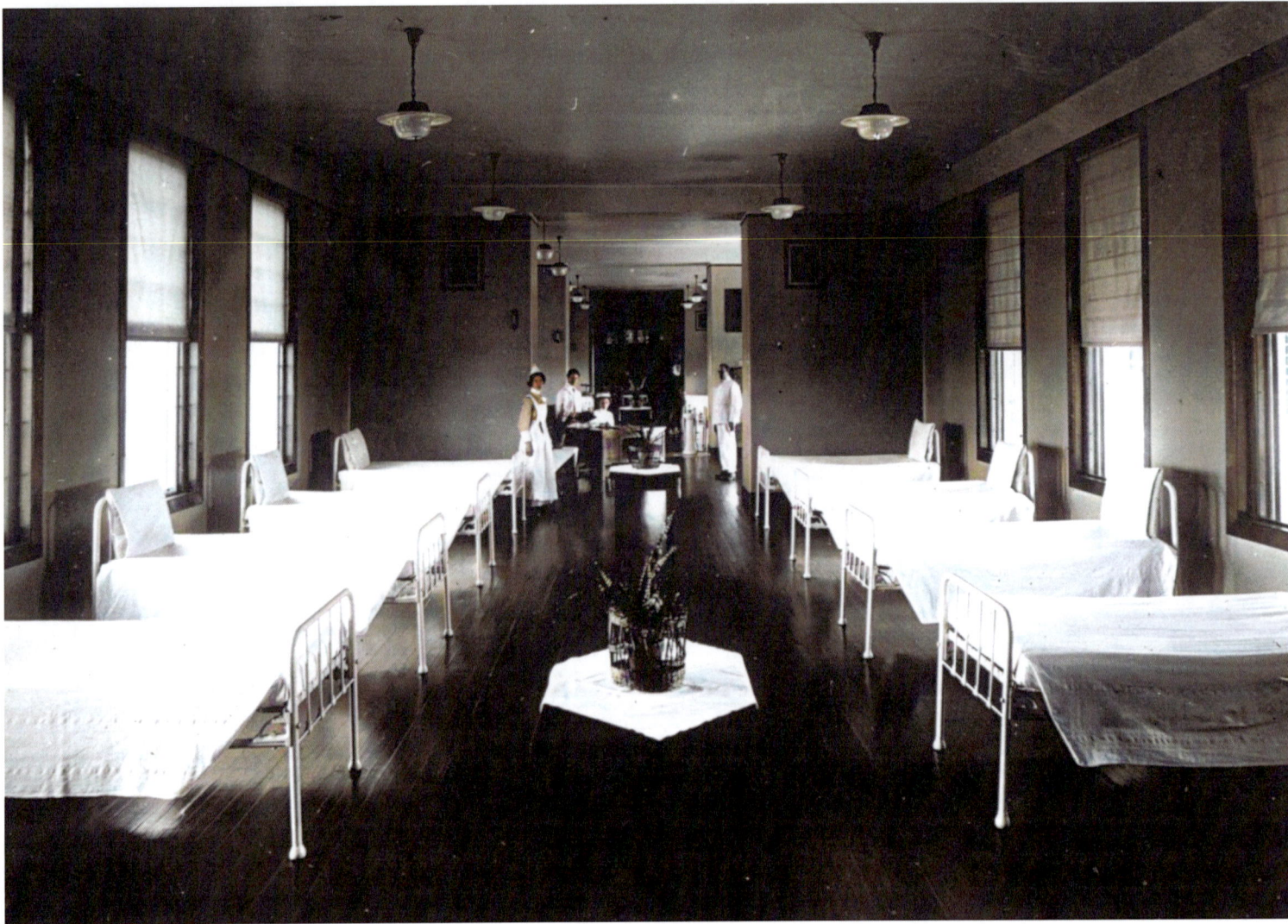

Reception Ward

Visiting Room

Patients Room

The Asylum for the Insane, now the State Hospital for Mental Diseases, is the largest of the group of institutions at Howard. In the year of which I write, about forty years ago, the Asylum, so-called, had a total of slightly over five hundred patients, about equally divided as to sex. The buildings were of rubble stone covered with cement. A twelve-foot high, tight, board fence enclosed the whole area, and, because of this, the institution was called the "sheep pen."

The fence line area extended westerly near where the present congregate dining room stands. Running southerly, the fence enclosed the laundry, and, terminating at the Boiler House, continued to Pontiac Avenue. Two large gates, one on each side of the phsyician's house, admitted coal teams into the yards on either side. The lamps, on posts stationed here and there throughout the yards, were common kerosene oil lamps. These, on dark nights, shed a small area of light around them, and, to traverse the yards without a lantern, was spooky, if not hazardous.

A strenuous attempt was made by the Superintendent to have the insane inmates, who were brought to the institution to be admitted, unshackled from the prisoners. This was protested by the sheriffs, who usually had the insane handcuffed to some prisoner, and many a scene of interest to the student of psychiatry was enacted in the admitting office.

Attempts to glean a history of the case from the admitting officer usually failed. They knew only the name on the admittance slip. There was no social worker with a case history, no stenographer to takes notes, no typist; the history gleaned from the patient was often disputed in its entirety when friends or relatives visited them.

The hard, straight-backed, long settees, where the ward patients sat all day, were placed back to back, and the attendant patrolled the ward like a sentry on his beat. Woe betide the inmate who sought liberty elsewhere than the bathrooms. During the winter months and during inclement weather, the "sit down" method was firmly adhered to. On fair days, a walk in the yard constituted the physical therapy. The patients were uniformed mostly in prison gray. Whether the brass buttoned, blue uniform of the North, and the gray suit of the inmates the rebel dress of the South, I know not.

The patient was made to feel, at the first contact with his or her attendant, that suppression of all violent and impulsive actions on his part would take place. There was no dearth of attendants, then. Most of them came from Maine; there was rarely one from Rhode Island. New York and Pennsylvania hospital attendants often were hired. Coming from older and more modern institutions, they brought with them the arts of subduing patients without bruising or "marking them up." Towel strangling, rubber rose beating and other refinements of cruelty were surreptitiously used.

State Hospital for the Insane, Female Convalescent Ward

State Hospital for the Insane, Male Convalescent Ward

State Hospital for the Insane, Stone Hall

Nurses Station

Steam Cabinets

Hydrotherapeutic Room

Sleeping Quarters

Bathroom

State Prison Boiler Room, Hospital, Kitchen, Mess-Room, Chapel

While it may be, and usually is, granted by the courts of Justice that a man is sentenced to prison to aid in his reformation, the principle back of it all is "Force," and this for the protection of the society which the prisoner has insulted. Sitting in his cell, viewing the massive masonry that detains him, there creeps in upon the prisoner, slowly and insidiously, the state of mind known as "prison psychosis," in which he dwells continually upon the plan as to how he can escape from his physical and mental enslavement and restraint.

Under the appellation of "Order and Discipline, and "Prison Regulations," the prisoner is made to lose his identity and personality as soon as he enters the prison regime. He is clipped, finger-printed, photographed and numbered, and, as a number, he is compelled by armed men to tread the dreary treadmill of prison routine. The ominous shadow of "Force" follows him everywhere. And if, while under the imperative impulses of escape, he flees, he is hunted by hound and men until his capture.

Then, to show him that his redemption must begin by the law of "obedience", he is furnished with a ball and chain to limit his escape impulses and those actions which are provided us by nature as "defense actions" (that is, fleeing from oppression) are thwarted by force. In order to distinguish him from those who submit to Rule and Regulation, he is clothed in a scarlet suit, a constant reminder that he is a conspicuous object, one who must be watched and noticed. To one of Napoleonic

ego, this very means was not a curative or reformatory method, but added all the more to a perverted sense of importance.

To some of these "Scarlet Runners", there was provided a form of punishment in the fields by making them stand upon a small stone, just large enough to limit them to standing perfectly still and straight upon it, and they were aided into an upright position by the boot of the guard if they dared to fall or lose their balance on their pinnacle of prominence. To further impress upon the resistant prisoner the power of those in authority, a form of mechanical torture was applied by means of a strait jacket, one of the most steady, drawing, pulling forms of force one could devise, and one which I found, in some marked instances, caused a traumatic neuritis of the shoulders which, because of its excruciating pain, brought the prisoner to medical attention on the sick line, often for months.

Because of this, the physicians insisted that no man should be so punished without an examination as to whether he could stand this form of punishment, and it was applied only in our presence. Under our orders, this form of punishment was finally abolished, as also was the bread and water diet.

The torture jacket, the black cell, the starvation diet, and the "numbered man" were gradually eliminated.

View of Corridor, State Prison

Prison Interior

State Prison Hospital

Setting Up Exercises, Sockanosset School

Chapel and Hospital, Sockanosset School

Cadet Officers of Battalion and Companies

Sockanosset School Cottages

The Sockanosset School was run on a military basis. Strict discipline was maintained, and, if abusive treatment was dealt out, it was without the Superintendent's sanction. He expected from his personnel sobriety and strict morality. Profanity and smoking on duty were not tolerated. If this, and a general letting down of morale and abuse crept in, it was after the decease of this sterling humanitarian.

It was most unfortunate for the general upkeep of the morale of the Reform School that they were the nearest neighbors to the State Prison and Providence County Jail. The boys came in contact with the Jail and Prison inmates in many ways. In emptying coal cars, they were in close company with those from the Jail. Many of these were "boys" who had served their minority at the School, and so great was the lure of these with their stories to the boys, that the latter would often express the wish that they could go to Jail and meet these heroic prisoners. These were an example to them, and they failed to realize that, in spite of all their cleverness, they had been caught and sentenced. Their sentences were, to them, always undeserved, and the result of the "cops" "persecuting them." These conversations often resulted in breaches of discipline by the elder boys at Sockanosset, and, when they became incorrigible, they were transferred to the Jail, where, as "men" they could be treated as men, have all the tobacco they needed, etc., and there be instructed by those steeped in criminality to advance further in the School of Crime.

There was practically no mental classification of the boys, and no psychometric examinations. If a boy became a stumbling block to others in his cottage, by reason of mental deficiency, he was finally sent to the State Almshouse, where the imbeciles and idiots were gathered together. This was before the establishment of the State School for the Feeble-minded at Exeter. But, long ere this occurred, he had been subjected to lay inspection and diagnosis, which often was founded upon stories of the boy's "laziness", "stubbornness", "faking", etc. After the lay treatment for these conditions had been tried and failed, then the physician's attention was called to the boy and he was transferred into another environment.

Blacksmith Shop

Exhibit of Work in Blacksmith Shop

Exhibit of Work in Carpenter Shop

Carpenter Shop

Mechanical Drawing

Exhibit of Work in Machine Shop

Oaklawn School for Girls

At the period of which I write, the Oaklawn School for Girls had a full house of fifty inmates. Eventually, the population increased to the extent that some provision would have to be made to segregate the younger, juvenile offenders, whose misbehavior was not too deeply criminal, from the older girls whose misdemeanors were of a deeper dye. The Eastman Cottage, for the younger children, was the answer to this problem, in 1908. The segregation was not complete, however, for contact was made daily in institutional matters.

The lessening of the physical contact, however, gave place to the isolation plan, which was to sequester the girl in her room, which had barred windows and solid doors. Here, alone, she could muse upon the episodes of the past, and plan how she would satisfy her biologic urge in the future without getting caught. The isolation cell, sometimes on the top floor, was the result of too much dormitory intrigue and love-making on the part of the girl.

To anyone now engaged in this work of juvenile reformation, The idea of spanking the bare bottom of a girl of sixteen to eighteen years of age, versed in the knowledge of the male sex, and a woman in all of her biological reasonings and demands, was certainly a demeaning procedure. The "turning them over on the lap and giving them a good warming" will appear to be a relic of the medieval past, as such it was, but the reader must reckon up the methods of that day when "taking the boy to the woodshed", the "razor strap", the "birch", and the "across the lap" method, the "boxing of the ears" and the "laying across the lap with the slipper" and the "shingle" were the accepted methods of parental discipline, and were, by the juveniles, the expected results of wrongdoing at their homes.

There were some juvenile reformers who felt that "the laying on of hands" in this personal, parental way was more efficacious than the "mechanical spanking machine" purported to be in use in some reformatories, when this was used, there was lost that personal contact of King and subject, the wonted "fillip" of personal satisfaction of well applied personal punishment.

It was a universal custom in the homes, and well appreciated there. It was, perforce, not too bad a custom to carry on in girls' reformatories for the "correction of those actions which, when pursued, would lead to the utter damnation of the soul and fix more firmly the incorrigibility of the one to be reformed." Thus argued those in charge. They only followed the light as they saw it.

Classroom

Sewing Room, Oaklawn School

Laundry, Oaklawn School

The supervision over this school, in its daily routine, was in the hands of a female Deputy Superintendent, later made Superintendent. She had been a ward matron-attendant at the State Almshouse, and was a robust, red cheeked widow, weighing well over two hundred pounds, whose complete fitness for the office of superintendent of a girls' school was a fair share of "common sense" and the ability to maintain order and discipline. Being an old fashioned, motherly soul, she relied upon old fashioned methods of spanking across her lap. As years crept on, this worthy woman became so corpulent that her lap was shortened by its rotundity, and her other asthmatic infirmities compelled her to resort to the use of woman's weapon, her tongue, and her burnings of the nether portions of these girls' anatomies were transferred to the higher, if not more impressionable centres, above the ears.

Under the direction of the Superintendent, the girls were instructed in calisthenics, dumb-bells, exercises, and those dances which were the vogue at that time. To impress the general public as to the progress these girls were making in the development of the body and those natural physical charms which so many of this type of girl possess, they had demonstrations in mass on the green lawn in front of the Superintendent's house, facing Pontiac Avenue.

In buggies and horse-drawn vehicles of every kind, the younger males came from the mills and farms nearby, and were regaled by the display of well-proportioned, twinkling limbs and the supple bodies, which displaced, in the minds of the gaping youths, the more bent forms and tired attitudes of the mill girls they escorted. This attitude of the admiring males was not lost on the "show girls", and they gloried in their charms and were stimulated by applause. Because of the increasing responsibility of the General Superintendent, a Female Superintendent was elected in 1909, and the general "showing off" of the girls was curtailed. Being a frugal housewife, and having had to toil in her younger years, the Female Superintendent believed in the doctrine of work. Under the tutelage of a matron who had a flair for horticulture, the larger girls were sent out in tan colored garments which well concealed their physical charms, and they were encouraged to develop their muscles by productive husbandry, as well as those domestic virtues of sewing, cooking, laundry, etc.

Physical Exercise, Oaklawn School

GIRLS AT WORK IN GARDEN, OAKLAWN.

Girls at Work in Garden, Oaklawn School

In The Garden

State Farm Inmates Building a Bank Wall

Workhouse and House of Correction

The proper term to designate this institution, where men were confined, and which was the only place where women prisoners were confined, even those committed to State Prison for murder, abortion, and grave crimes, was "The State Workhouse and House of Correction."

The term "State Farm" was loosely applied. It became a sheriff's idiom. It meant that prisoners, committed for petty crimes, such as "drunkenness," "lewd and wanton," and "vagrancy," were usually designated as State Farm prisoners.

The female prisoners, sent here by the courts, were from all walks of life. Many of them hid their family names under aliases, and had been, in some instances, when they were young and fair, respectable young women.

Under the beguilement of some male, who, in the days of their innocence, they loved, they were seduced, and, from the shame consequent upon this, they dropped out of the family group. They went to other places to work and live, and oft saw, in the daily press, their own physical features described among the list of "missing persons." Step by step, down the corridor of degradation they went, usually accompanied by someone better versed in the practice of crime than themselves. Friendly procurers, male and the more dangerous female, were near them to aid in their sale or barter into the houses of low amusement or of prostitution, and, under the rule of domination of these procurers, they were sold or exchanged from city to city. As their good looks and attractiveness of person diminished, the use of alcohol and drugs to stimulate their flagging powers were often resorted to, and when, to this, the diseases in the form of gonorrhea or syphilis were added, they sank lower into the quagmire of crime and dissipation, and finally fell into the hands of police.

In some instances, if good looks had not wholly departed, they were bailed out of the House of Correction by their "friends" in whose debt they were and forever would be, until they were no longer of service to their bondsmen because of disease or drunken degradation. They became the worthless chattel, the cast-off refuse of their soul and body-destroying environment.

This refuse of humanity the Women's House of Correction sought to work up into usefulness. After treatment for alcoholism or the drug habit, these unfortunate women were placed in positions doing sewing and darning, until, through medicine, good food and rest, they were well enough to be put into laundry work, house-keeping, dormitory work, etc. In most instances, it was surprising what good food and rest accomplished toward their physical restoration. The change in their mental make-up was slower. While their protestations against their former mode of life were apparently sincere, officials felt there was a long, hard, up-grade pull to make ere they reached the quieter plateau of rehabilitation.

Ironing

Laundry

Sewing

Sewing Circle

Making Shoes

Making Toys

Kitchen

Shop

State Almshouse

Leaning heavily upon the text of Holy Writ that "the poor ye have with ye always," our forefathers evidently considered that there would always be plenty of them and there was but little use to greatly improve their condition.

It is, therefore, no surprise to find at Howard, in 1893, a large, overcrowded building, full of the pitiable poor. As a result of the startling revelations of Thomas Hazard of Narragansett, who wrote to the Rhode Island Legislature years before of the people chained in attics, corn cribs, outhouses, barns, etc., there was a transferring from homes and such places of the feeble-minded, the frenzied epileptic, the low-grade idiots, and the unwanted feeble and aged relatives to their respective town or county almshouse, or so-called "Poor Farms." These, in turn, saw to it that the State was far better fitted to care for this class than the "poor farms", and they transferred to the State Almshouse at Howard their most undesirable inmates.

As a result, the State Almshouse was a lazaretto of the worst cases in the State. The worthy poor, the aged man and wife, separated at the door, were in close companionship, in wards with the tubercular, the syphilitic, the feeble-minded, the pregnant, the illegitimate infants, the idiots, and the morally vicious. The bedridden, suffering from every known disease, accumulated. Overcrowding developed rapidly. The feeble-minded, the idiots, the morons, and the ambulatory aged were crowded into the ill-lighted and not well ventilated basements, soon to become worse from the lack of pure oxygen and sunshine.

Attempts at a proper segregation of these classes were strenuously employed and succeeded only in part. The buildings were always filled, and the ambulatory cases paid little attention to sanitation cups, and their germ-laden sputum was expectorated over walls and the bits of lawn in the yard, there to be smeared onto the shoes and the clothing of the imbeciles and others who were able to traverse the yard.

Long before Wallum Lake, many of the tubercular cases were Bravos, great, muscularly-built men, who, coming to this El Dorado – to them, God's country – to make their fortunes, found in their environment and the damp atmosphere the harbinger of death. They died in large numbers.

Likewise, the handsome, Irish immigrant girls, with glossy black hair and beautiful eyes and complexions, in working as domestics were peculiarly susceptible to tuberculosis. Here at Howard, far from the home they loved – the beloved Green Isle of Erin – in a strange land and without friends, they died rapidly from tuberculosis, consoled by the clergy and by the last rites of the Church, and mourned by the attendants and the baffled physicians, who saw their once beautiful forms, now emaciated with disease, laid in the alien soil of the Potter's Field.

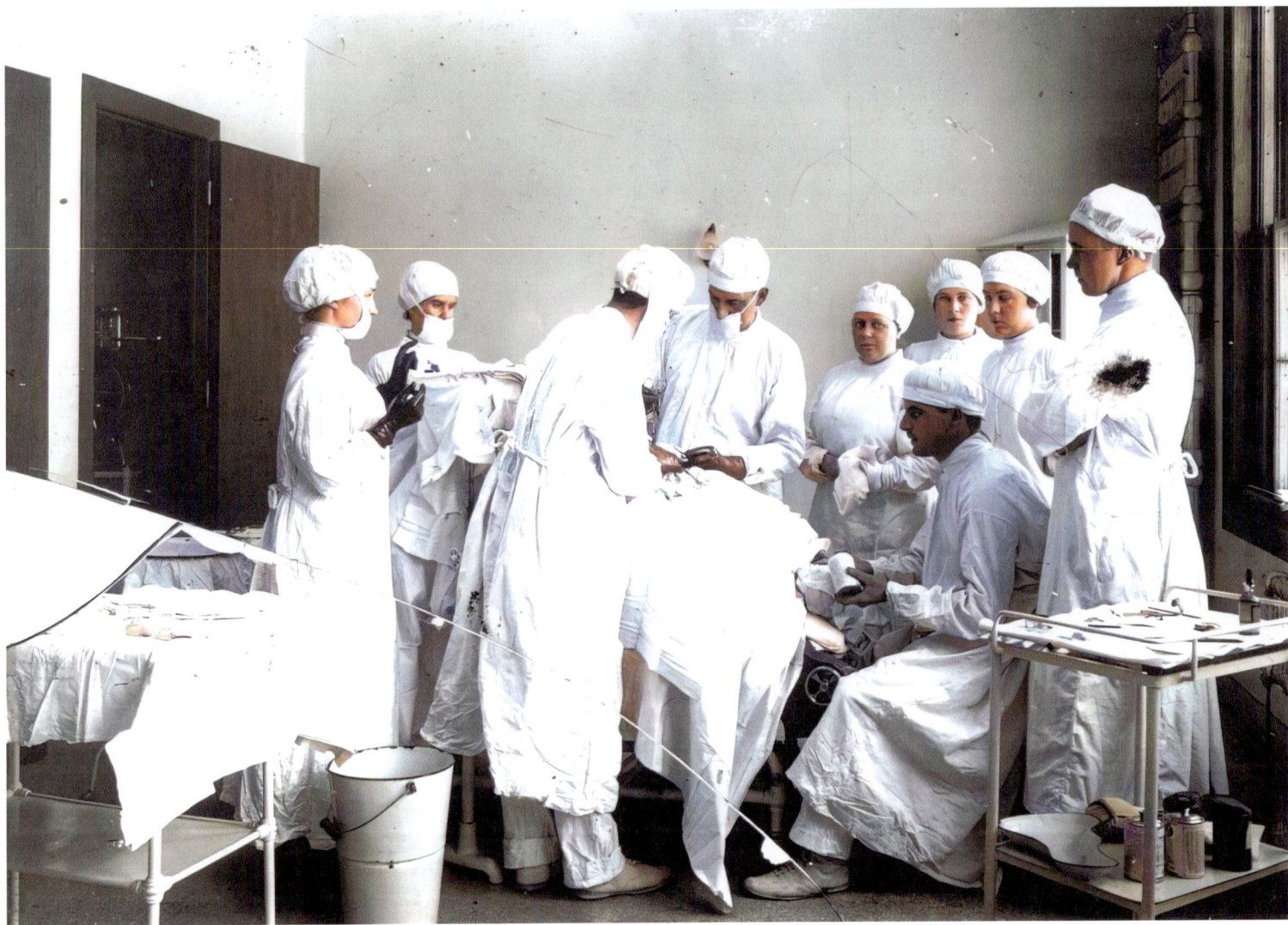

Operation

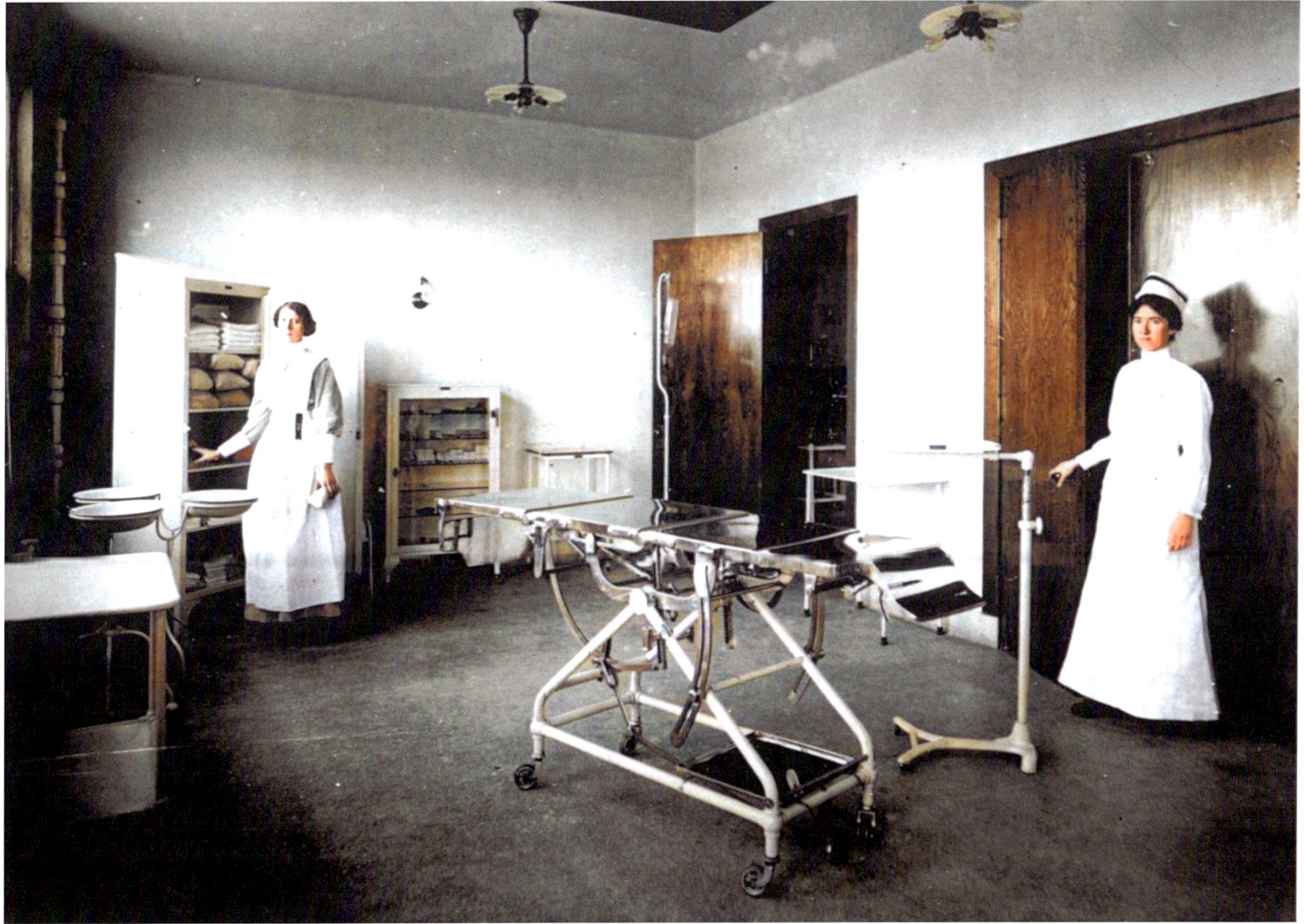

Operating Room

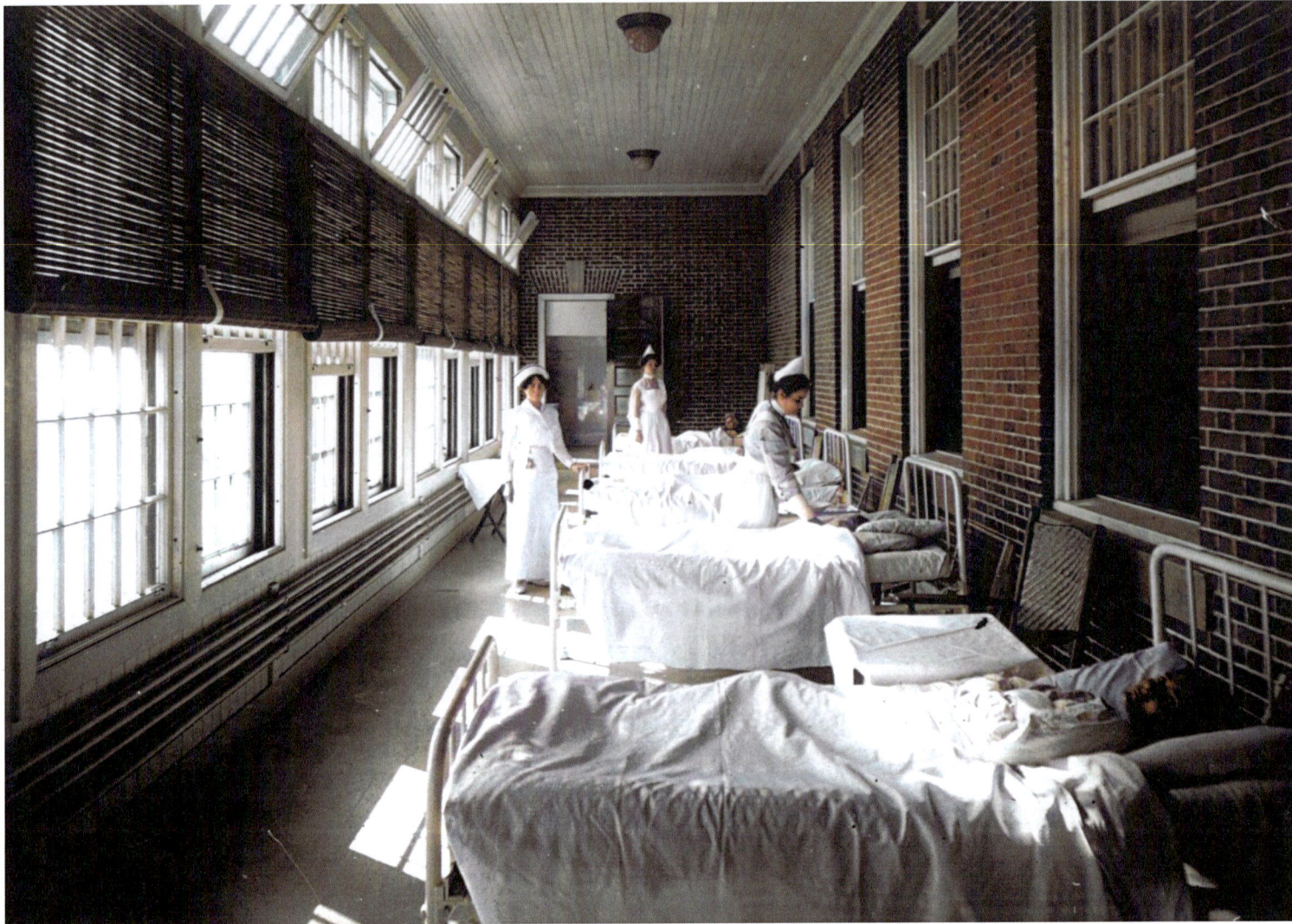

Sleeping Porch

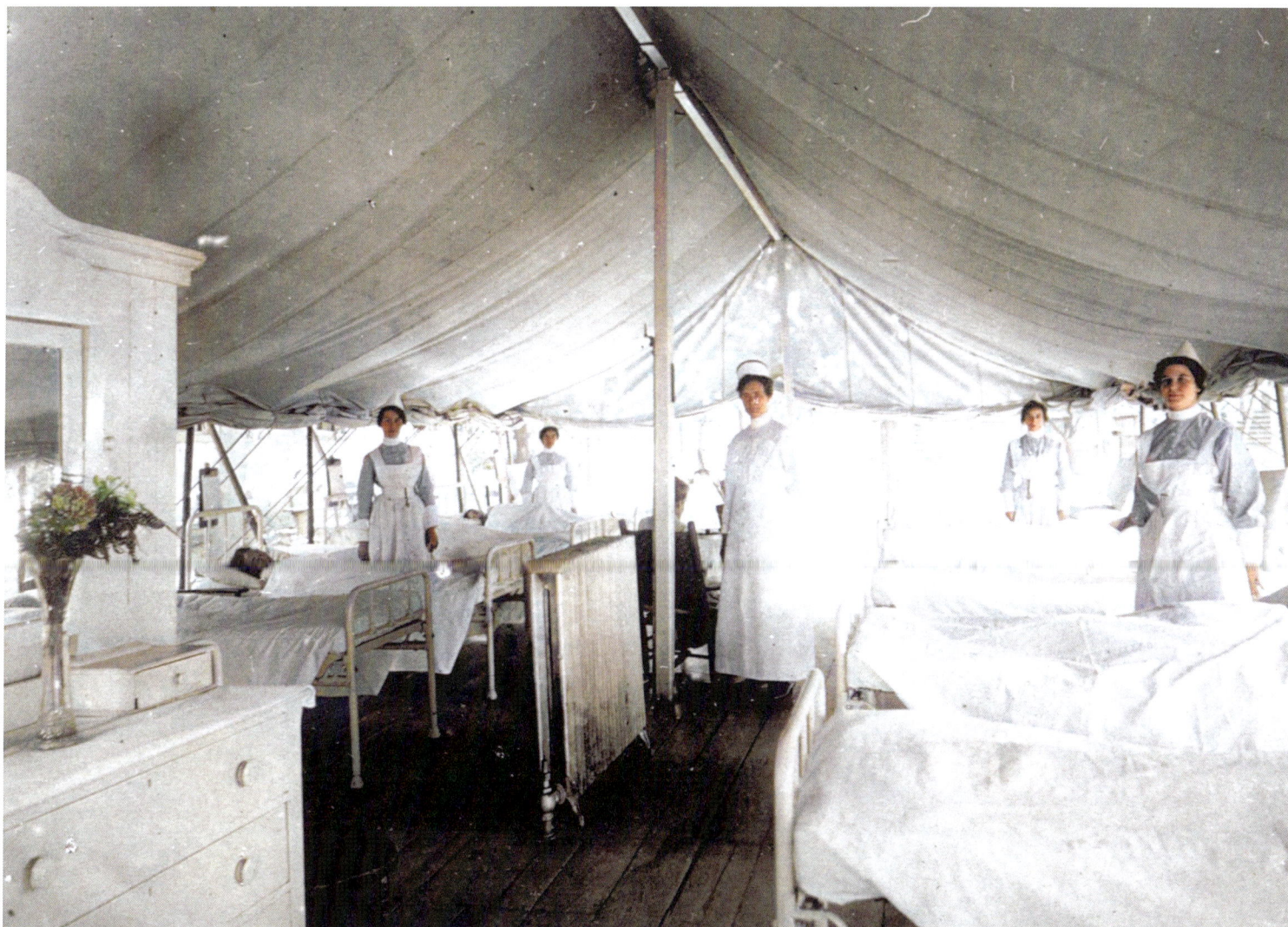

Tuberculosis Tent

Picnic

Greenhouse

Entrance, State Institutions at Howard

Hospital for the Insane, State Institutions at Howard

Benches at the State Farm

Fence at the State Hospital for the Insane

State Institutions Entrance Gate, Dec 27, 1900

As I stand now, in 1942, upon the fragments and ashes of what was once that depot of misery and sorrow, I see again once more that sad scene. It is forever engraved upon the cylinders of my memory, and I hear once again the flute-like song of that bird, radiating a hope against the lowering sky, and I am glad to say that I have lived to see the clouds part, break up, and partly disappear. I hear clearly, the song of "Hope" continued, and the name of Howard to me no longer rings out like the tocsin of despair, but is a name that now means a healing of the bodies, the minds and the souls of those who, through their own frailties, or the sins of others, plead with us to bear them up, to forgive them their trespasses, to heal their broken minds and bodies; and the name of Howard to them will no longer bear the stigma of the past, but be as a beacon of hope to those oppressed in sorrow or estate. It is a name reflecting to them the mercies of God applied to them by those skilled in the arts of healing, and, through these agencies, they find in the term, Howard, a name synonymous with Hope, a name emblazoned in gold on the banner of their State.

As I stand there upon the remnants and ashes of the past, I have seen emerging from these ashes, great hospitals, the lessened cruelty, and the more humane and comprehensive understanding of the whole plan of social welfare. I no longer hear the cry of the strait-jacketed prisoner. I no longer hear the clang of the ball and chain. No longer does the scarlet-suited prisoner dot the landscape and catch the eye as if it were the mark of Cain. Looking and pondering upon these things, and seeing how those in authority in the legislature view this great problem with a greater understanding and humane interest, I realize that the world is a better world than it was; Howard is a much better place than it was, and though once it was the stone in social welfare that the builders rejected and threw away, it has become, in truth, the cornerstone of a greater social welfare program than has ever been.

Never again, by the grace of God, will the intelligence of the State be insulted by the things of the past nor by that legend once over Howard that was written over Dante's Inferno: "Leave Hope behind, all ye who enter here."

State Hospital for the Insane

Howard, Rhode Island.

www.ingramcontent.com/pod-product-compliance
Lightning Source LLC
Chambersburg PA
CBRC101827090426
42811CB00024B/1922